Wisdom & Wisecracks for the
Aspiring Business Owner

Copyright © 2009 Will Estell
Beach Mountain Press; IMG Books
All rights reserved.

ISBN 1-4392-1486-7
ISBN 13 978-1439214862
Library of Congress Control Number 2008909403

To order additional copies, please contact us.
BookSurge
www.booksurge.com
1-866-308-6235
orders@booksurge.com

Wisdom & Wisecracks for the Aspiring Business Owner

Will Estell

2009

Dedication

To Aime and my children

The four of you are the inspiration behind every positive action I take.

The book's finished; let's go to the beach.

1

The first rule is, Never Stop Dreaming.

2

The second rule is, **Stop listening to those who tell you to "stop dreaming".**

3

Reality is a place for those who have forgotten how to dream.

4

If the advice of naysayers is so valuable, how come it's free?

5

Most of the people who will tell you to "slow down and take your time" still haven't gotten anywhere.

6

"If it were that easy everybody would be doing it" is a quote used in self justification by those who don't even care to try.

7

Listening isn't really the key to success.
It's knowing who to listen to.

8

"Job Security" is often a term used to explain, "I've been here miserable for years and haven't had the courage to do anything about it".

9

Remember, when receiving negative comments, from co-workers, about starting your own business; "misery loves company"...and lots of it!

10

"**H**ate" isn't a negative thing if it promotes positive change.

11

Change does not take time. It takes dedication. Decide to do it and begin to make it happen that very instant. It really IS that simple.

12

To fail because of not trying is far worse than to be successful while doing nothing at all.

13

When taking advice about beginning your business don't ask a life-long company worker.

14

Jobs are created for people who can't create their own.

15

Careers are sometimes jobs that are simply harder to leave.

16

"**A**dvance your career" sometimes means "make it even harder to leave the job you already dislike".

17

If money really is the motivating factor that leads to happiness in any and all jobs; how do you explain miserable millionaire CEO's?

18

If "Loving what you do" was really the determining factor to financial success, then lazy overweight couch potatoes would all be rich...there is a bit more to it.

19

Getting up for work is a lot easier when your boss is sleeping with you.

20

Time is something that flows much faster when it's all yours.

21

Success, in business as in life, is what happens while we are busy overcoming failure.

22

Failure is simply part of the learning curve on the way to success.

23

Belief in yourself is equally important as belief in your service or product. Both are necessary elements to your success.

24

Life is what passes you by while you put all of yours into someone else's business or dream.

25

Prosperity is what you create when you decide to take control of your own destiny...and you **DO** have the power to take control.

26

Going into business without a detailed plan is like taking a cross-country trip without a **GPS**. You may ultimately end up at the right place but the trip won't be near as pleasant.

27

Working for yourself requires a lot of self discipline; make sure you are willing to follow your own directions- while also maintaining an open mind to the advice of certain others.

28

Determine quickly who these "certain others" really are and your business success will come much sooner.

29

Working for someone else is great...if you really believe in their dreams more than yours.

30

Balance is what you must achieve in order for your business to work for you- rather than you working for your business.

31

Eighty hours per week with no time for family, friends or a life is not the ideal "dream". Think about this when planning your particular business model.

32

When deciding to start your own business think carefully which one you really want to be in; to often people simply choose one that they think will produce more income. You need to actually enjoy what you do to be truly successful.

33

Ability to run a particular business doesn't always mean it's the right business for you. That's like believing that an ability to do math means you should be an accountant. Think first…think hard.

34

Starting your own business should provide some freedom from the less favored aspects of what you currently do, or did, at your job…if it doesn't maybe you should rethink the business.

35

Before deciding on a business type, first decide what aspects of business ownership most appeal to you (time, money, flexibility); these vary greatly with different businesses.

36

In business, the better the fit, the better the results.

37

There is no rule that says you can't be involved in more than one business at the same time. Twice the odds of succeeding? Maybe, but the opposite could also be true...so, be very careful.

38

Paying too much attention to the so called "rules of business" can sometimes hin-der your ability to actually succeed.

39

Vision is something you can gain as you research any given venture; sometimes it will lead you in the direction you were looking in, sometimes it will lead you away.

32

Pay close attention to the numbers, even in your planning stages.
Note: Didn't you already read number 32?

Close attention!

41

When selling a service or product, being the "**BIG** fish in a little pond" is not necessarily important as long as you can figure out a way to sell to the other ponds too (i.e. internet, auction sites, wholesalers).

42

The ability to laugh at your own mistakes isn't funny if you make the same ones over-and-over.

43

Intelligence in business isn't as easily identified as a diploma on the wall...just ask Bill Gates or Steve Jobs; neither of them have one.

44

A love for what you do helps a lot; a love for who you are is a necessity.

45

A waiter is someone who thinks money grows on trays. A restaurant owner is someone who knows money grows on goals.

46

Tomorrow is a place that gives you the opportunity to begin changing the rest of your life.

47

Yesterday is where you were.
Tomorrow is where you are going.
Today is a bridge between the two; cross it.

48

Encouragement from family and friends is fuel to help you believe in yourself. Dreams and desire are the catalyst that can turn that belief into reality.

49

Investments from others into your business are like billboards that say, "We really believe in you".

Make sure you continue to see, read and believe these "signs".

50

If you must take on investment partners, only take silent ones. Active partners only make sense if they already know more than you about your particular type of business.

51

When taking on any investor(s) **NEVER**- Yes, that's **NEVER**- give up the majority of control- unless it is the **ONLY** way possible.

52

Your own business without being in control is like...well, working for someone else.

53

Be wary of people actively soliciting working partners for an already established business; often they only want your investment in hopes of salvaging an already diminishing venture.

54

When considering buying into any existing partnership, look very closely at all of the numbers...over and over, and with professionals who know what to look for. There can be a very fine line between a good deal and a very bad one; make sure you find it before crossing it.

55

Instead of learning the "tricks of the trade",
spend time really learning the trade.

56

Be careful when dealing with "Angel" investors...remember, Satan was an angel once too.

57

Borrowing money to make money always makes sense...just be sure you know how to make it first.

58

Life is too short to be miserable, but too long to simply be content.

59

Be very careful in handling your business finances; be even more careful when letting someone else handle them.

60

Be willing to take constructive criticism from your business peers. Learning about their mistakes may keep you from making the same ones yourself.

61

Remember that in business, the lack of money and other resources can often be the birth of ingenuity.

62

Also remember, money doesn't really solve problems, smart people solve problems.

The more of these you initially surround yourself with the less money you will often need.

63

The old adage "Do what you love and the money will come" is only true if you have enough money to wait.

64

In determining your business' goals make sure they will eventually allow you to also meet your own.

65

If you are a female in business, don't be offended that some men may give you what you want, or be more agreeable in dealing with you, simply because you are a woman. Using this to your advantage is no different than a man using his charm, smile, or a good suit to his advantage.

66

Being seen as attractive -whether you are a man or a woman- isn't a bad thing. Business is tough; if you have an advantage, by all means use it.

67

When using appearance, gender or intelligence to your advantage, know that there is a fine line as to how far these may get you and how often you should utilize them.

Find that line before you cross it.

68

Never use ethnic, gender, educational or financial background as an excuse why you -or anyone you know- cannot achieve great success in business or in life.

Ask Oprah Winfrey, Suze Orman, or Barack Obama if it stopped them.

69

When deciding on your type of business think about what products or services others really want; instead of simply what your interests are...if they can be combined, even better.

70

Find a "hunger" for a particular product or service then provide that product or service. All too often people beginning businesses go about this in exactly the opposite way.

71

Avoid choosing a product or service that you don't have a sincere interest or belief in. Selling under those circumstances essentially requires lying to your potential customers.

72

A product or service that has no real long term need will likely not fuel a long term business either.

73

Be careful of fads or trends in any product(s) or service(s).

Due to the short term nature of their cycle they should never be your primary source of business revenue...in other words, when the fad is over, so likely may your business be

74

Know your primary target market: who they are, what age group they are in, their interests and spending habits; learn to think much as they do. With this knowledge you will truly be able to reach and service your customers in the best way.

75

Remember that in retail and web businesses—especially those involving clothing, music, electronics, and accessories- the highest spending demographic are the 13 to 25 year olds. This group will directly influence the success of any business in these categories; get to know them.

76

Once you learn to think like your customers, you will be able to influence them to think like you.

77

"The customer is always right"...isn't always right.

Learn to realize when right is alright, and when to call them "wrong".

78

In business, as in much of life, the one who keeps his or her "cool" most often comes out on top.

79

Being argumentative with a customer is like fighting a war...
in the end no one totally wins.

80

Once in business you will find that many others need your business to support theirs (ads, products, services)...Just be careful not to make their business successful at the cost of breaking yours.

81

When choosing a place for your retail or service business, remember three important things: Location. Location. Location.

82

When choosing an internet based or supported business, remember these three important factors: Traffic. Traffic. Traffic.

83

The best web site in the world is worthless
until enough people know it is there.

84

Don't be afraid to locate yourself near your potential competitors...there is a reason that most McDonald's, Wendy's and Burger King restaurants are in sight of each other.

85

Play your cards right and your competitors can actually become your best source of generating traffic. People like to shop and we have become a society dependant on having choices.

86

Advertising is an essential part of **ANY** new business.

It will often be the most important factor in generating your initial traffic. Many businesses live or die based upon 'the right' advertising.

87

Be very careful when choosing where to advertise that you choose the medium most viewed, heard or read by your specific target demographic. Advertising money is a waste if spent reaching the wrong people... no matter how many of them you reach.

88

Thinking you can save money by not advertising is like thinking you can stop time by not wearing a watch.

89

Always treat your employees with the respect they deserve, and they all deserve some.

90

The best way to show appreciation to your employees is to simply tell them, "I appreciate what you are doing".

91

When you are working for yourself, never forget what it feels like to work for someone else. This is a primary key in surrounding yourself with good employees who sincerely care about your business.

92

Good productive employees are hard to find; once you find them do all you can to keep them.

93

Remember that your employees are human and they are going to make some mistakes...just like you.

94

Be careful when thinking of hiring family and friends; if the business relationship goes south the other may go with it.

95

Remember that no one is going to care as much about your business as you do, but if you find someone that is close, keep them that way...close.

96

Once in business for yourself, moms and dads should always remember, "The people you **REALLY** work for are waiting for you at home".

97

The greatest balance to be achieved in life or business is that of time;

Learn to efficiently manage this and everything else will soon fall into place.

98

Never grow your business at the expense of shrinking your family.

99

Be careful to never take part in a business venture that you would be embarrassed for your children to be involved in…because they will be by association.

100

Shady businesses often have big returns, but only in terms of money. Remember that your business impacts you and your family much more than simply monetarily.

101

The most valuable asset of your business will often be your integrity.

102

Learn to be open-minded to new money making opportunities, but careful not to jump into "hot new ventures" with claims of huge returns and nothing to back them up by those attempting to sell you.

103

The old adage, "If it sounds too good to be true, it probably is", isn't always true...just most of the time.

104

Opportunity knocks...but it normally doesn't ring the door bell, blow up the phone, spam, and paste flyers all over the place.

105

Be wary of people who always seem to have the newest "best opportunity ever"- two or three times per year.

Nobody gets that lucky that often.

106

Sometimes the best business opportunity is the one you are now pursuing.

107

Even the best organizations with the best products or services don't actually make everyone who sells for them rich. There needs to be a "fit" between you and your product or service.

108

Be careful not to get blinded by hype...
even your own.

109

Often all of the confusion in MLM organizations is done just for that reason...to confuse. Get all the facts, figures and realistic projections before paying to be involved.

110

Be aware that many wealthy and famous business people offering to sell you advice have gotten that way...well, just by selling their advice.

III

Name 5 people who are well known for offering business, success, or life changing advice through infomercials, books, or seminars. Now name how each of these persons acquired their fortune. See. Funny, isn't it?

112

Remember, your advice and knowledge could be worth something to someone too; especially if you actually earn it first-hand.

113

The first person to learn from your misadventures and mistakes in business should always be you.

114

In business, as in life, making mistakes is inevitable...

Not learning from them is just stupid.

115

Replication is often the key to long term business success...carefully choosing what to, and not to, replicate is the determining factor.

116

If business success could be learned from simply reading a book...I would have written that one instead of this one.

Now it's up to you; read, research, plan and make it happen. It won't be all fun and games, but if you like to play there's no better game to win, than that of owning and growing your own business.

To Success!

-Will

Acknowledgements

To all of the men and women who have kept the American Dream alive by continuing to believe in themselves, their individual ideas, goals, and dreams and the belief that each and every one of us- no matter who we are- can obtain the level of success we desire.

Whether your definition of business success is buying and managing an existing retail or service company, designing and selling a new clothing brand, starting a race team or event promotions company, or being the next multi-millionaire commercial property mogul...your goals are obtainable if you believe in yourself enough to make your dreams a reality, and it is because of all of you who dare to dream, create, and succeed that there is a reason for this book.

I would also like to say "Thank You" to all of those who have believed in me and have been there to boost my confidence and help maintain my focus in all of my adventures, ventures...and even misadventures. It is because of God, family, friends, and business mentors that I have learned enough to conjure up these original thoughts and tips, and put them into print.

A special thanks goes out to: my wonderful wife and children for all of their patience and understanding while "Dad is always working"; all of my parents (Estells, Mays and Towne) for…well, everything; all of my brothers and sisters (Yes, you too Beth & Stephen); my longtime friend, Tom Buzan for sharing his years of life and business wisdom; Jim Ulrey for his advice and time when I was buying my first brick and mortar business -never underestimate how small gestures of time and wisdom can leave a lasting impression on those you help, Thank you my friend; Jeff Borrelli, President of Integrated Media Group, for your encouragement and friendship; Jenny Legun, Senior Publishing Consultant at Amazon's Booksurge; Jason Ruhf and Lindsey Usher, Manuscript Managers at Booksurge and everyone who facilitated in bringing this book to fruition.

I could've done it without some of you, but it would've been a lot more difficult and taken longer…Gotcha!